JESUS IN HIS OWN WORDS

A LAYMAN'S PERSPECTIVE

John Matthew

Jesus in His Own Words:
A Layman's Perspective
© 2021
Trinity House Publishers

CONTENTS

INTRODUCTION

Using only the spoken words of Jesus Christ recorded in the Bible, the purpose of this book is to offer a greater understanding of the central figure of Christianity (and in all of human history) and to demonstrate the significance of his message. From a layman's perspective, I give brief analyses of his words, illuminating their context and/or amplifying their meaning. Although I have no formal theological training, I am a follower of Jesus, and I read Scripture and other Christian literature regularly.

As I was attempting to discover what Jesus said on particular subjects, I found some difficulty locating the Scripture passages that were most applicable. Thus, I began compiling those verses which I thought most powerful in understanding him and then organized them in such a way so as to be useful to others in addition to myself. This book is the result of those efforts.

As I work on the final edits of this manuscript, I realize that I began this project in November 2019. Interestingly, that was the date that my then-eighteen-year-old grandson, Will, was diagnosed with acute leukemia and later a rare form of lymphoma, a combination so rare that there is no known cure. In the intervening months, Will has been fighting for his life, spending the majority of his time in three different hospitals. He is truly the most courageous person I have ever known; he never complains nor does he give up. His parents are constantly at his side providing him love and care. The pain they too experience is unimaginable. I believe that God set the idea of this book on my heart, and that this is Will's book. We continue to have faith in God, regardless of the suffering that we endure, as we know and understand that he is always there for us.

Fortunately, for the past twenty-five years, I have had the great opportunity to attend a weekly men's Bible study taught by one of the world's foremost theologians and biblical scholars, Dr. Kenneth Boa (for more enlightenment visit www.kenboa.org). Ken has been the inspiration for many of the explanations put forth in this manuscript. At my request, he reviewed and edited the material to fulfill our desire to create an accessible resource that anyone can understand but that is still theologically accurate.

GOALS

I hope this book will be helpful to both those who believe in Jesus and those who simply want to learn a bit more about who he is. For those of you who consider yourselves believers, this is a quick and easy reference manual of the important things that Jesus said, organized by topic. If you are simply interested in learning about Jesus but don't want to get bogged down in hard-to-understand theological jargon (I must admit to wanting to avoid that difficulty myself), or if you find the Bible somewhat overwhelming, this book is for you. You will find a simple and organized review of the words of Jesus so that you can better understand him, his message, his purpose on earth, and why his words are of importance to everyone.

In that regard, perhaps this book will create an interest in Jesus that will lead to further study. As C. S. Lewis so succinctly notes, "Christianity, if false, is of no importance, and, if true, of infinite importance. The one thing it cannot be is moderately important."[1]

I believe Lewis is right, and I hope you will come to the same conclusion.

THE APPROACH

I highlight key verses of the Bible that record words spoken by Jesus (indicated in red type). These passages are mostly from the Gospels (the first four books of the Bible's New Testament)—Matthew, Mark, Luke, and John; however, I also include a few verses from the books of Acts and Revelation. There are a total of 201 focus passages.

Following each passage is a brief comment that seeks to amplify, clarify, and contextualize Jesus' words, but without diminishing the profound nature of his statements. In some instances, portions of a verse are omitted in order to focus on the key message of the text. If you have a Bible available to you, I encourage you to read the complete text as well as the preceding and subsequent verses. (I have used the ESV Bible translation in this book; the NASB1995 is another good translation.)

This book certainly does not contain the entirety of the recorded words of Jesus, as the purpose is to highlight his most significant words to afford the reader a concise understanding of Jesus and his importance. Due to the sheer volume, not all of Jesus' teachings are captured in this book. Neither do I offer in-depth theological analysis of the Gospels. However, my hope is that this presentation is comprehensive and compelling enough so as to spur further study and exploration of Jesus and his words, and of the entire Bible. By presenting explanations in layman's terms, I seek to imitate the Gospel writers (Matthew, Mark, Luke, and John). Writing in the language of the people, those authors were not highly educated religious scholars but ordinary working men—including a fisherman (John), a tax collector (Matthew), and a physician (Luke). By contrast, the apostle Paul, writer of many of the other books in the Bible's New Testament, carried impressive credentials, including training under one of the foremost teachers and experts in Jewish law of his time.

Passages are organized topically first rather than chronologically. To really grasp the importance of Jesus, we must start with statements regarding his deity—that is, his claim to be the Son of God. This topic is followed by other ways Jesus describes his identity; his purpose on earth; prophecy (which anticipated his arrival); his miracles; key teachings on life in the kingdom of God; words to his disciples; key prayers; and his trial, crucifixion, and resurrection. I conclude with Jesus' words about salvation, the end times, and final judgment. Although the sequence of topics is meaningful, you can certainly read the chapters in a different order than they are presented. For example, you might find inspiration by first reading chapter 5, which explores some of Jesus' core teachings on the ways of the kingdom of God.

A tremendous amount of theology is packed into these 201 passages—truths about God that are important to each of us. I hope you find this book to be a helpful guide in your own journey.

The Author
January 2021

1

HIS IDENTITY

The name of Jesus is known throughout the entire world, and most people understand that he is the central figure in the Christian faith (indeed, the very name "Christian" means "little Christ," stemming from Jesus' call for people to follow him as his disciples). Not everyone agrees with all that Scripture says about him, but few argue against his teachings on love, compassion, humility, forgiveness, and avoiding sin (i.e., anything contrary to the character of God). Nevertheless, we cannot embrace these latter parts of his teaching without also considering what he says about his own identity. Indeed, perhaps the most contentious aspect of Jesus' teaching is what he says about himself. So let's begin our exploration with those claims.

~

HIS DEITY

Who is Jesus? A mere mortal? Or the immortal God himself, in human form? Perhaps you have heard some people say something like this: "Yes, Jesus was a man who lived two thousand years ago; he was a great moral teacher and prophet who gave us wise counsel. However, I have trouble accepting the claim that he is God." In light of such common skepticism, let's review Jesus' own words and see what he says about his relationship to God.

As you will see in the following passages, he claims to be the Messiah—the long-awaited deliverer of God's people, anticipated in the Hebrew Bible. He also claims to be the Son of God and to be one with the Father. As C. S. Lewis says, someone who makes these kinds of statements cannot be merely a good moral teacher. In fact, Jesus leaves us with only three choices. He is either a lunatic (a condition which has not been put forth even by his most ardent critics), a liar (something few people would claim based on his good moral teaching), or, if he is telling the truth, the Lord himself.[2]

Jesus' own statements make it clear that he considered himself not only from God but also (based on certain texts) fully God. The Jewish leaders in Jesus' day considered some of his statements totally offensive. They also were infuriated by the attention he drew and the challenge he posed to their own power and authority. Thus, they sought to put him to death. So, consider the following passages, and ask yourself: What is he—a lunatic, a liar, or God? There are no other options.

∽

"I and the Father are one." (John 10:30)

This is total heresy to the Jewish leaders, who respond, "It is not for a good work that we are going to stone you but for blasphemy, because you, being a man, make yourself God" (v. 33). Clearly to the Jewish leaders, Jesus is calling himself God. This is very important: Either Jesus is speaking the truth or Jesus is a madman! These Jewish leaders would have considered this claim (and many of the others on the following pages) outrageous.

❧

"Whoever has seen me has seen the Father." (John 14:9)

Again, Jesus is stating that he and the Father are one. The apostle John describes this oneness in the opening chapter of his Gospel as follows: "In the beginning was the Word, and the Word was with God, and the Word was God. He was in the beginning with God" (John 1:1–2). (The term "Word" refers to Jesus in this passage.)

❧

"I who speak to you am he." (John 4:26)

Jesus says this after a Samaritan woman has said, "I know that Messiah is coming (he who is called Christ). When he comes, he will tell us all things." In his response, Jesus is affirming that he is truly the Messiah foretold in the Old Testament.

❧

"I came from God and I am here. I came not of my own accord, but he sent me." (John 8:42)

This is another strong statement from Jesus, offering no ambiguity as to his true origin.

✼

"My teaching is not mine, but his who sent me." (John 7:16)

His words, his works, and his teachings are directly from God, his Father.

✼

"No one has ascended into heaven except he who descended from heaven, the Son of Man." (John 3:13)

The term "Son of Man" is the most common way in which Jesus describes himself. In the Old Testament, Daniel 7:13–14 also uses it to describe the Messiah.

✼

"You have seen him [the Son of Man], and it is he who is speaking with you." (John 9:37)

Jesus is explaining to a once-blind man, to whom he has just given sight, that he is the Son of Man.

✼

"Do you say of him whom the Father consecrated and sent into the world, 'You are blaspheming,' because I said, 'I am the Son of God'? If I am not doing the works of my Father, then do not believe me; but if I do them, even though you do not believe me, believe the works, that you may know and understand that the Father is in me and I am in the Father." (John 10:36–38)

After the Jews accuse Jesus of the blasphemy of calling himself God's son and thus God also, he responds by saying that the miracles he has performed demonstrate that he is telling the truth and that he is who he claims to be.

He is also stating that he and the Father are one, a mystery that is revealed in the New Testament. As it becomes increasingly clear in the rest of the Bible, there is a third person in the Godhead, the Holy Spirit. These three persons—Father, Son, and Spirit—are mysteriously united as one while also distinct from each other, dwelling in communion together. The term used to represent this concept about God is the Trinity (however, the word "Trinity" is never used by Jesus or stated in the Bible).

※

"The works that I do in my Father's name bear witness about me." (John 10:25)

Jesus is referring to the miracles that he has performed, which indicate his divine powers.

※

"All things have been handed over to me by my Father, and no one knows the Son except the Father, and no one knows the Father except the Son and anyone to whom the Son chooses to reveal him." (Matthew 11:27)

Jesus boldly calls God his Father and states that the Father sent him to do his works. Jesus is describing his unique relationship with God. To be the Son of God in this sense would make Jesus God also.

~

HIS DESCRIPTIONS OF HIMSELF

We learn much about Jesus through the ways in which he describes himself. He clearly states his deity; that he was sent to earth to give us guidance, hope, and protection; and that through him we will find salvation—that is, eternal life with God in heaven. The terms he uses to describe himself are not ones we would expect in casual conversation. They are powerful, and all are noteworthy. Particularly important in understanding Jesus' identity are his seven "I AM" statements in the Gospel of John.

"I am the bread of life." (John 6:35)

The children of Israel ate "manna" (bread-like food from heaven) every day in the wilderness, but they eventually died. Jesus provides more than physical bread; he offers true spiritual food that leads to eternal life.

"I am the light of the world." (John 9:5)

Jesus came to counteract the darkness of the world and give us the privilege of sharing in his light.

"I am the door. If anyone enters by me, he will be saved." (John 10:9)

There is no other "door" to God besides Jesus. Anyone can enter through this door, but it requires faith in him to do so.

"I am the good shepherd." (John 10:11)

Just as a shepherd cares for his sheep, Jesus cares for us, even laying down his life for us.

"I am the resurrection and the life." (John 11:25)

Jesus is claiming to be the wellspring of spiritual and biological life. To believe in him is not merely to acknowledge that he rose from the dead, but it also involves receiving his gift of resurrected life. Faith in him is more than believing a proposition; it is a transfer of trust from ourselves to him.

"I am the way, and the truth, and the life. No one comes to the Father except through me." (John 14:6)

Jesus is the way to salvation—he speaks only the truth, and eternal life can be found in him alone. Interestingly, the early church was called "the Way."

※

"I am the true vine." (John 15:1)

Just as a vine brings nourishment to the fruit, so as branches of the vine, we receive his life and thus bear spiritual fruit. Apart from the vine, the fruit withers and dies; this is an apt metaphor for our need to abide in Jesus.

※

"I am gentle and lowly in heart." (Matthew 11:29)

We can find peace and rest in Jesus, as he gives us respite in our sufferings. We too are to be gentle and humble to others as we follow his example.

※

"I who speak to you am he." (John 4:26)

After the Samaritan woman who gives Jesus water at the well says that she understands that the Christ prophesied by the Old Testament will come, Jesus affirms that he is the Christ. This is a profound statement and leaves no ambiguity as to who he claims to be.

※

"I am from above.... I am not of this world." (John 8:23)

Jesus is clearly stating that his origin is from God. Although he was born of an earthly mother, we learn in Luke 1:35 that he was conceived by the Holy Spirit. The eternal one who made all things entered into his own creation with undiminished deity but also full humanity, so that he is now the unique God-man.

※

"Before Abraham was, I am." (John 8:58)

God the Father describes himself as the great "I AM" in Exodus 3:14. In John 8, Jesus describes himself in the same manner. He is also stating that he was there with the Father before the beginning of time. In fact, when God said, "Let us make man in our image" (Genesis 1:26), he used the plural "us" rather than the singular "me," indicating that he was not alone. Based on later revelation (e.g., John 1), we can conclude that Jesus was with his Father at the creation.

※

"I am the Son of God." (John 10:36)

To the Jewish leaders, Jesus' claim to be the Son of God was heretical because it elevated Jesus to the level of God himself.

2

HIS PURPOSE

Christ reveals himself throughout his earthly life as the Savior sent by the Father for the salvation of the world. His very name, "Jesus," expresses this mission, as it is translated "the Lord saves."

If we seek only the promises of the world, we will never be totally satisfied in this life, and we will never get to experience the joy of heaven. However, if our focus is to please God, we will find joy both here on earth and (to an even greater degree) when we unite with Jesus in heaven.

Through Jesus, we have the opportunity to join him in heaven for eternity. By heeding his call to turn from dependence on ourselves to entrusting ourselves to him, we too can find eternal life.

※

"Why were you looking for me? Did you not know that I must be in my Father's house?" (Luke 2:49)

This is our first glimpse of the young Jesus at age twelve as he responds to his parents (Mary and Joseph). Separated from them, the young Jesus was actually sitting in the temple court learning from the teachers and asking them questions. Those who were there were astonished at the insight and wisdom of this young man. We know nothing of his life after this until he begins his ministry about twenty years later. This early incident demonstrates Jesus' early awareness of his unique purpose as the one sent by the Father to fulfill the Scriptures.

❦

"The kingdom of God is at hand; repent and believe in the gospel." (Mark 1:15)

Repentance means turning away from ourselves and turning to Jesus for the grace of forgiveness and new life. Without genuine belief and trust in him, we will never enter God's kingdom.

❦

"What are you seeking?" (John 1:38)

This is the first question Jesus asks in his public ministry, and our answer to this question reveals the most important thing about us. We are defined by what we desire. As Peter Kreeft writes in *Christianity for Modern Pagans*: "The great divide . . . is not between theists and atheists, or between happiness and unhappiness, but between seekers (lovers) and nonseekers (nonlovers) of the Truth (for God is Truth). . . . We can seek health, happiness, or holiness; physical health, mental health, or spiritual health . . . [but] Christ's first question in John's Gospel is the crucial one. . . . This question determines what we will find, determines our eternal destiny, determines everything."[3]

※

"The Son of Man has authority on earth to forgive sins." (Mark 2:10)

Only God can forgive sins. Therefore, Jesus, as the Son of God (and one with the Father), has the authority to forgive us of our sins.

※

"Everyone who drinks of this water will be thirsty again, but whoever drinks of the water that I will give him will never be thirsty again. The water that I will give him will become in him a spring of water welling up to eternal life." (John 4:13–14)

Speaking to the Samaritan woman at the well who had drawn water for him, Jesus offers "living water." Using the metaphor of water, Jesus is telling us that the drink—that is, the life-giving sustenance he offers—will satisfy us forever.

※

"For this reason the Father loves me, because I lay down my life that I may take it up again." (John 10:17)

His primary purpose on earth was to give his life as a sacrifice to cover the guilt and shame of humanity. He would endure the agony of death, but it would not defeat him, because he would rise up out of the grave on the third day.

※

"Do not think that I have come to abolish the Law or the Prophets; I have not come to abolish them but to fulfill them." (Matthew 5:17)

Jesus introduces a major shift in the religious requirements laid down by the Jewish leaders of his day. Whereas these leaders placed great importance on the outward observance of the law, claiming that one could enter heaven by such observances, Jesus teaches that the requirements of the law go much deeper, to our inner thoughts and motives. Only Jesus himself is able to keep God's law perfectly, and therefore we must trust in him—not in our good works—for salvation.

※

"If anyone hears my words and does not keep them, I do not judge him; for I did not come to judge the world but to save the world. The one who rejects me and does not receive my words has a judge; the word that I have spoken will judge him on the last day." (John 12:47–48)

Jesus, at his first coming, came as our Savior, not to accuse, condemn, or judge any person, including those who defied God and persecuted him. He has reserved that judgment for when he returns.

※

"For judgment I came into this world, that those who do not see may see, and those who see may become blind." (John 9:39)

Although Jesus did not come to judge the world in the sense of condemnation, his message does judge the heart in terms of reception—some will seek the truth while others will seek to avoid it. In this verse, Jesus refers to spiritual sight ("the light," as he calls it elsewhere). Those who suppose that they see are actually blind, but those who acknowledge their desperate condition before God are the ones who actually see.

⁜

"For the Father judges no one, but has given all judgment to the Son. . . . Truly, truly, I say to you, whoever hears my word and believes him who sent me has eternal life. He does not come into judgment, but has passed from death to life." (John 5:22, 24)

As mentioned earlier, the first time he came to earth, Jesus did not come to condemn but to save. In his second coming, however, he will judge all people, and those who follow him will share eternity with him.

⁜

"Whoever would be first among you must be your slave, even as the Son of Man came not to be served but to serve, and to give his life as a ransom for many." (Matthew 20:27–28)

Jesus' followers thought that the Messiah had come to be their king, one who would lift them out from under the repression of the Roman rulers. An earthly king is served, but Jesus is not an earthly king. He is a heavenly king who came to earth to serve all people, even to the point of becoming a living sacrifice for us to ransom us from our sin.

❖

"I have said these things to you, that in me you may have peace. In the world you will have tribulation. But take heart; I have overcome the world." (John 16:33)

In this life, we deal with the trials of sickness, tragedy, natural disasters, and violence. However, by faith in Jesus, we are able to walk through adversity with peace and purpose, because we know Jesus will be victorious over the sins and injustices of this world. As his followers, we will share that victory with him. Notice, this does not mean we will be able to escape adversity—in fact, Jesus promises trouble will be a part of our earthly existence.

3

HIS FULFILLMENT OF PROPHECY

Jesus is the fulfillment of scores of biblical prophecies. Moses, Daniel, Isaiah, David, Micah, Zechariah, Samuel, and others all spoke of him. In fact, the whole Hebrew Bible (Old Testament) points to the coming of the Messiah. Here are some of the prophesied details: the virgin birth in the town of Bethlehem from the lineage of David; the ministry of his forerunner, John the Baptist; his miracles; hatred by the world; his arrival in Jerusalem on a donkey; his betrayal for thirty pieces of silver; abandonment by his friends; his crucifixion, with no bones broken but his hands and feet pierced; the lots his captors cast for his clothing; and, most significantly, his resurrection. It defies statistical probability that one man would fulfill these and many other prophecies.

Jesus additionally foretold events that came to pass during and after his lifetime on earth: Judas's betrayal, his (Jesus') own trial and crucifixion, Peter's denial of him, and the destruction of the temple (the center of Jewish worship in Jerusalem). The accuracy of his predictions is further evidence that he is who he says he is.

Jesus also described how the world would look after his ascension into heaven, and he warned us about the forces with which his followers would have to contend. Jesus' descriptions of his crucifixion, his resurrection, the end times, and his return appear in chapters 10 and 12.

⚜

"This is he of whom it is written, 'Behold, I send my messenger before your face, who will prepare your way before you.' Truly, I say to you, among those born of women there has arisen no one greater than John the Baptist." (Matthew 11:10–11)

John the Baptist, a cousin of Jesus, preceded Jesus in proclaiming that the people should repent of their sins, and he baptized multitudes in the river Jordan. This was prophesied in Malachi 3:1.

Interestingly, when the pregnant Virgin Mary visited her cousin Elizabeth (John the Baptist's mother), the unborn John (several months older than Jesus) leapt in Elizabeth's womb, demonstrating the spiritual bond between John and Jesus.

⚜

"Let it be so now, for thus it is fitting for us to fulfill all righteousness." (Matthew 3:15)

Before Jesus begins his ministry, he instructs John the Baptist to baptize him, just as John had been doing to others. As Jesus comes up from the water, heaven opens, and a voice from heaven says, "This is my beloved Son, with whom I am well pleased" (v. 17).

※

"Elijah has already come, and they did not recognize him, but did to him whatever they pleased. So also the Son of Man will certainly suffer at their hands." (Matthew 17:12)

Jesus is referring to John the Baptist, as Hebrew prophecy maintained that Elijah was to return before the Messiah came (Malachi 4:5). Elijah was a key Old Testament prophet who, in one instance, proved the existence of the one true God and dramatically struck down the prophets of a false god (1 Kings 18). Jesus is saying that John the Baptist represented Elijah as the one who prepared the way for him. And as John suffered, Jesus too would suffer.

※

"If you believed Moses, you would believe me; for he wrote of me." (John 5:46)

Moses (the most prominent prophet of the Old Testament and the one whom God used to deliver his people out of slavery in Egypt) prophesied the coming of Jesus when he said, "The LORD your God will raise up for you a prophet like me" (Deuteronomy 18:15).

⚜

"Today this Scripture has been fulfilled in your hearing." (Luke 4:21)

After reading from Isaiah 61, which prophesies the coming of the Messiah, Jesus states that he is the fulfillment of that very prophecy. This would be a shocking statement for those listening to him in the synagogue in his hometown of Nazareth.

⚜

"Go into the village in front of you, and immediately as you enter it you will find a colt tied, on which no one has ever sat. Untie it and bring it. If anyone says to you, 'Why are you doing this?' say, 'The Lord has need of it and will send it back here immediately.'" (Mark 11:2–3)

Jesus spoke these words to his disciples in his last days, before entering Jerusalem (where he would be arrested and condemned to die). The verses describe how Jesus was about to fulfill the prophecy of Zechariah 9:9, which specified that the Messiah would ride into Jerusalem on a colt of a donkey.

⚎

"The light is among you for a little while longer. Walk while you have the light, lest darkness overtake you. The one who walks in the darkness does not know where he is going. While you have the light, believe in the light, that you may become sons of light." (John 12:35–36)

Jesus is saying that he (the light) will not be on earth much longer, as he will be in heaven until he returns a second time. He warns his listeners that they should walk as children of light in the midst of a dark world.

⚎

"Did I not choose you, the twelve? And yet one of you is a devil." (John 6:70)

"Truly, truly, I say to you, one of you will betray me." (John 13:21)

In conversation with his disciples, Jesus indicates that one of them, Judas, will betray him to facilitate Jesus' capture. This happens just as predicted.

❧

"Truly, truly, I say to you, the rooster will not crow till you have denied me three times." (John 13:38)

After Peter says he will lay down his life for Jesus, he is rebuked by Jesus' words about what will really happen after Peter is accused of association with Jesus. In fact, Peter will deny knowing Jesus on the night of his betrayal by Judas.

❧

"The ruler of this world is coming. He has no claim on me, but I do as the Father has commanded me, so that the world may know that I love the Father." (John 14:30–31)

Jesus explains that the enemy will have power over this world but not over him or those who have believed in him.

❧

"For the days will come upon you, when your enemies will set up a barricade around you and surround you and hem you in on every side and tear you down to the ground, you and your children within you." (Luke 19:43–44)

"Truly, I say to you, there will not be left here one stone upon another that will not be thrown down." (Matthew 24:2)

Jesus weeps as he foretells the coming destruction of Jerusalem, including its temple, which would actually take place in AD 70.

※

"You know that after two days the Passover is coming, and the Son of Man will be delivered up to be crucified." (Matthew 26:2)

Jesus predicts exactly when he will be captured, tried, and executed. Interestingly, his disciples could not really understand the gravity of what was about to happen. This is not the first time Jesus predicts his death.

※

"You will all fall away because of me this night. For it is written: 'I will strike the shepherd, and the sheep of the flock will be scattered.'" (Matthew 26:31)

Quoting Zechariah 13:7, Jesus tells his disciples that they will abandon him when confronted with his captors. Tragically, that is exactly what happens.

※

"Have you come out as against a robber, with swords and clubs to capture me? Day after day I sat in the temple teaching, and you did not seize me. But all this has taken place that the Scriptures of the prophets might be fulfilled." (Matthew 26:55–56)

Jesus is speaking as he is being taken prisoner, explaining that his capture was prophesied in Zechariah 13:7: "Strike the shepherd, and the sheep will be scattered."

⁂

"O foolish ones, and slow of heart to believe all that the prophets have spoken! Was it not necessary that the Christ should suffer these things and enter into his glory?" (Luke 24:25–26)

After his resurrection, Jesus speaks to two disciples on a road headed toward a town called Emmaus (about seven miles from Jerusalem), reiterating the need for the Christ to suffer for their sins to be forgiven. The two disciples don't recognize that it is Jesus speaking to them until he reveals it at the blessing of the bread before a meal. This is one of multiple post-resurrection appearances.

⁂

"Thus it is written, that the Christ should suffer and on the third day rise from the dead. . . . You are witnesses of these things." (Luke 24:46, 48)

After his resurrection, Jesus encounters his disciples on the shore of the Sea of Galilee and explains to them that he has fulfilled the Old Testament prophecy about himself.

4

HIS MIRACLES

The Gospels describe dozens of miracles performed by Jesus. A few examples include the following: He raised the dead, walked on water, calmed a violent storm, cured leprosy, made the blind see and the lame walk, fed thousands with a few loaves of bread, and removed demons from the possessed. Only the Son of God could do such things, and Jesus performed these miracles for the purpose of demonstrating his divine powers so that the people might believe that he is who he claims to be. As he himself says: "Believe me that I am in the Father and the Father is in me, or else believe on account of the works themselves" (John 14:11).

"Woman, what does this have to do with me? . . . My hour has not yet come." (John 2:4)

This is an excerpt of a dialogue that precedes Jesus' first miracle at the wedding of Cana. The father of the bride is in a bit of an embarrassing situation, having run out of wine at the wedding celebration. So, Mary, the mother of Jesus, asks her son to help, and he turns gallons of water into wine. Although none of the guests are aware of what has happened, they all lavish praise on the host for providing the very best wine at the end of the party (when hosts usually brought out the lowest-quality wine). This is a great metaphor for the fact that the best is yet to come.

※

"Be silent, and come out of him!" (Mark 1:25)

Jesus casts out the spirit of a demon-possessed man in the synagogue. The demon actually recognizes Jesus and calls him the "Holy One of God."

※

"Be clean." (Mark 1:41)

Jesus heals a man with leprosy.

※

"Go; your son will live." (John 4:50)

After a man hears that Jesus has arrived in Galilee from Judea, he goes to him and begs him to come and heal his son, who is close to death. Jesus does not even have to visit the man's house but heals the son from a distance.

⚜

"Get up, take up your bed, and walk." (John 5:8)

At the pool of Bethsaida, a man has been an invalid for thirty-eight years. When Jesus sees him lying there, he cures his disability, and the man gets up and walks away.

⚜

"I say to you, rise, pick up your bed, and go home." (Mark 2:11)

As Jesus is speaking in a crowded room, some people lower their friend, a paralytic, on a mat through the roof, and Jesus immediately heals him.

⚜

"Peace! Be still!" (Mark 4:39)

Jesus calms a storm as he and his disciples are crossing the Sea of Galilee. As God, he has power over nature and the elements.

⚜

"Come out of the man, you unclean spirit! . . . What is your name?" (Mark 5:8–9)

Jesus drives out a multitude of demons (named "Legion") in a possessed man. They know the power of Jesus and beg him to allow them to enter a herd of swine (which he grants). But the swine run into the lake and drown; thus, all the neighbors ask that Jesus leave, as they want no part of someone who could ruin their livestock and means of living.

⚜

"Daughter, your faith has made you well; go in peace, and be healed of your disease." (Mark 5:34)

Jesus speaks with a woman in a crowd who touched his cloak; her belief in Jesus led to her immediate healing from a malady from which she suffered for twelve years.

⚜

"Why are you making a commotion and weeping? The child is not dead but sleeping. . . . 'Talitha cumi,' which means, 'Little girl, I say to you, arise!'" (Mark 5:39, 41)

Jesus brings back to life the daughter of a synagogue leader. The neighbors all laugh at him when he says she is only sleeping, as they know she is dead. He quickly proves his point as he commands her to get up, which she does to the joy of her parents and the shock of the neighbors.

⚜

"According to your faith be it done to you." (Matthew 9:29)

Jesus restores eyesight to two blind men, who responded affirmatively to his question, "Do you believe that I am able to do this?" (v. 28), demonstrating not only his power to do miracles but also the power of their faith in him.

⁂

"Go and tell John what you hear and see: the blind receive their sight and the lame walk, lepers are cleansed and the deaf hear, and the dead are raised up, and the poor have good news preached to them." (Matthew 11:4–5)

This is Jesus' answer to the disciples of John the Baptist when they ask if he is the Messiah. Jesus' simple reply is that his works confirm that he is the prophesied Messiah.

⁂

"How many loaves do you have?" (Mark 6:38)

Jesus has been teaching a large crowd in a remote place and has compassion for their needs. So he asks his disciples how many loaves of bread they have. With only five loaves and two fish, he breaks the bread and feeds a crowd of five thousand men (not counting women and children), with twelve baskets left over.

⁂

"Take heart; it is I. Do not be afraid. . . . O you of little faith, why did you doubt?" (Matthew 14:27, 31)

Approaching their boat while walking on water, Jesus calms the fear of his disciples.

❦

"I have compassion on the crowd, because they have been with me now three days and have nothing to eat. And if I send them away hungry to their homes, they will faint on the way. And some of them have come from far away." (Mark 8:2–3)

For a second time, Jesus feeds a large crowd while teaching in a remote area—this time with seven loaves of bread and a few fish. Again, there was an abundance beyond their needs, with seven basketfuls left over.

❦

"It was not that this man sinned, or his parents, but that the works of God might be displayed in him." (John 9:3)

Jesus responds to a question from his disciples as to why a certain man was born blind. They wonder if his infirmity is because of the sin of his parents. Jesus explains that this condition occurred in order that he could perform the miracle of restoring the man's sight, so that others could see this and believe in him. After saying this, Jesus heals the man.

❦

"Lazarus, come out." (John 11:43)

Jesus raises Lazarus from the tomb on the fourth day after he had died. This miracle astonishes all the local residents (in the town of Bethany), and word quickly spreads to the Jewish leaders in Jerusalem, further stoking their anger.

5

HIS TEACHINGS:
THE WAY OF THE KINGDOM

Jesus gives us wisdom on what it means to live a life that is pleasing to God. The apostle Paul summarizes some of these principles in his letter to the Colossians: "Put on then, as God's chosen ones, holy and beloved, compassionate hearts, kindness, humility, meekness, and patience, bearing with one another and, if one has a complaint against another, forgiving each other; as the Lord has forgiven you, so you also must forgive. And above all these put on love, which binds everything together in perfect harmony" (3:12–14).

~

THE BEATITUDES

Jesus taught the Beatitudes during his famous Sermon on the Mount. These eight declarations of blessing embody the essence of the spiritual life and describe the benefits of the attitudes and actions they prescribe. Some behaviors encouraged in the Beatitudes are ones that we may already strive for: mercy, a hunger for righteousness, purity of heart, peacemaking. Others are difficult for us to accept: being poor in spirit, mournful, and meek. But perhaps the most striking of these blessings is the eighth, which says that if we are persecuted because of our belief in Jesus, we will be truly blessed.

⁂

"Blessed are the poor in spirit, for theirs is the kingdom of heaven." (Matthew 5:3)

We are to acknowledge our spiritual bankruptcy before God.

⁂

"Blessed are those who mourn, for they shall be comforted." (Matthew 5:4)

A proper response to our spiritual bankruptcy is mourning our sinful condition. But this mourning will be replaced by comfort.

⁂

"Blessed are the meek, for they shall inherit the earth." (Matthew 5:5)

In God's economy, the humble will be lifted up.

❧

"Blessed are those who hunger and thirst for righteousness, for they shall be satisfied." (Matthew 5:6)

Those who have an appetite for the things of God will be filled.

❧

"Blessed are the merciful, for they shall receive mercy." (Matthew 5:7)

Because God treats us with mercy (not giving us what we deserve), we should treat others better than they deserve.

❧

"Blessed are the pure in heart, for they shall see God." (Matthew 5:8)

The pure in heart desire one thing above all else—the ultimate good of knowing God.

❧

"Blessed are the peacemakers, for they shall be called sons of God." (Matthew 5:9)

When we have peace with God, we can pursue peace with others.

ॐ

"Blessed are those who are persecuted for righteousness' sake, for theirs is the kingdom of heaven." (Matthew 5:10)

As Paul puts it, "All who desire to live a godly life in Christ Jesus will be persecuted" (2 Timothy 3:12). From an earthly point of view, this appears to be counterintuitive, but Jesus is speaking of the eternal glory that our temporary sufferings will produce.

∼

DEALING WITH SIN AND TEMPTATION

Sin is anything that is contrary to the character of God. It manifests in innumerable ways in our thoughts, words, and deeds. Temptation is not sin but can lead to sin.

ॐ

"Let him who is without sin among you be the first to throw a stone at her." (John 8:7)[4]

The Pharisees bring a woman to Jesus and say, "Teacher, this woman has been caught in the act of adultery. Now in the Law, Moses commanded us to stone such women. So what do you say?" (vv. 4–5). They are testing Jesus to see if he will suggest that they ignore the law, which required that she be stoned to death. After he challenges them with this statement, they all walk away, realizing no one is without sin. Jesus then tells the woman to go and sin no more.

☙❧

"Repent, for the kingdom of heaven is at hand." (Matthew 4:17)

Jesus inaugurated his teaching with these words near the Sea of Galilee. His teaching in this region was a fulfillment of prophecy in Isaiah 9:1–2. Because of sin, changing our direction (repentance) is required.

☙❧

"Watch and pray that you may not enter into temptation. The spirit indeed is willing, but the flesh is weak." (Mark 14:38)

Although these are words that Jesus spoke to Peter in the Garden of Gethsemane, they are applicable to us today. We may want to do the right thing, but the pull of selfish thoughts and desires can be powerful. That gravity is always present, but by trusting in Jesus and depending on his Spirit, we can overcome this downward pull.

❧

"For from within, out of the heart of man, come evil thoughts, sexual immorality, theft, murder, adultery, coveting, wickedness, deceit, sensuality, envy, slander, pride, foolishness. All these evil things come from within, and they defile a person." (Mark 7:21–23)

Jesus is responding to criticism about eating certain impure foods and states that the source of sin is not what we eat but what comes out of our hearts. The problem is not external but internal.

❧

"You have heard that it was said, 'You shall not commit adultery.' But I say to you that everyone who looks at a woman with lustful intent has already committed adultery with her in his heart." (Matthew 5:27–28)

By moving beyond outward actions to inward thoughts, Jesus raises the standard, because even those who have not committed the physical act may still be guilty of adultery. By the same token, all of God's commandments become unattainable when our thought life is taken into account.

~

PRACTICING FORGIVENESS

The basis for forgiving others is realization of the depth of our own forgiveness by God. Because of Jesus' sacrificial death, God does not treat us with justice (giving us what we deserve) but with grace (giving us better than we deserve). In the same way, he commands us to treat others in a way that is better than they deserve.

※

"Father, forgive them, for they know not what they do." (Luke 23:34)

Jesus desires forgiveness for those who mocked him and hung him on the cross. What an extraordinary example of forgiveness: Jesus even forgives those who tortured and crucified him!

※

"For if you forgive other people their trespasses, your heavenly Father will also forgive you, but if you do not forgive others their trespasses, neither will your Father forgive your trespasses." (Matthew 6:14–15)

Forgiveness is essential for a follower of Jesus. Choosing not to forgive others reveals a failure to grasp the depth of our own forgiveness by God.

⁂

"I do not say to you seven times, but seventy-seven times." (Matthew 18:22)

When asked by his disciples how many times one should forgive those who transgress against us—"Lord, how often will my brother sin against me, and I forgive him?" (v. 21)—Jesus responds by saying one should essentially forgive indefinitely: Forgive and keep on forgiving. Forgiving someone does not mean we have to forget the past and trust that person in the future. To forgive the culprit is to deal graciously with that person just as Jesus does with us.

⁂

"In anger his master delivered him to the jailers, until he should pay all his debt. So also my heavenly Father will do to every one of you, if you do not forgive your brother from your heart." (Matthew 18:34–35)

Jesus tells the parable of the ungrateful manager, whose master forgave his own debts, but who refused to forgive the debts of his servants. When the master discovered the duplicity of the manager, the master reversed his prior decision and punished the manager as the manager had punished the servants. The lesson of this parable is that a failure to forgive others is an indicator that we may not truly grasp the forgiveness God has extended to us.

⁂

"Everyone who is angry with his brother will be liable to judgment.... First be reconciled to your brother." (Matthew 5:22, 24)

We are called to seek reconciliation with those who have provoked us. This is a clear call to forgive—and a clear warning against holding grudges or harboring unreconciled anger and bitterness toward others.

⁂

"And he said to him, 'Son, you are always with me, and all that is mine is yours. It was fitting to celebrate and be glad, for this your brother was dead, and is alive; he was lost, and is found.'" (Luke 15:31–32)

In this parable of the prodigal son, the father is explaining to the obedient son why he is rejoicing that the "lost" son has returned and sought redemption. Likewise, many are lost, and we should give them mercy as they renounce their sins and seek forgiveness. Ken Boa says of the power of forgiveness, "Not to forgive is like drinking poison and waiting for the other person to die."[5]

~

JUDGING GRACIOUSLY
True judgment depends on self-awareness—of our own position before God and of our need not only to receive but to display grace in our attitudes toward others.

"Judge not, that you be not judged. For with the judgment you pronounce you will be judged, and with the measure you use it will be measured to you." (Matthew 7:1–2)

We can and should be discerning about others and hold people accountable for the laws of society. However, final judgment is reserved for Jesus, who will judge perfectly.

"How can you say to your brother, 'Let me take the speck out of your eye,' when there is the log in your own eye? You hypocrite, first take the log out of your own eye, and then you will see clearly to take the speck out of your brother's eye." (Matthew 7:4–5)

We are usually much quicker to judge the faults we see in others than our own. Oftentimes, in fact, we discern a very small offense in another much more quickly than a larger one in our own life. Jesus isn't saying that we should never point out others' faults, but we will never be able to do so with accuracy and love while we are ignoring our own sins and shortcomings.

~

LOVING GOD AND OTHERS

We're called to love God completely (with all our heart, soul, mind, and strength). As we do so, we are able to love ourselves correctly by seeing ourselves as he sees us instead of as the world sees us. When God defines us as part of his family, we are secure enough to love and serve others.[6]

"A new commandment I give to you, that you love one another: just as I have loved you, you also are to love one another." (John 13:34)

"This is my commandment, that you love one another as I have loved you. Greater love has no one than this, that someone lay down his life for his friends." (John 15:12–13)

Here, Jesus tells his disciples the importance of loving others in the way we love ourselves. This "new commandment" is a much greater standard because his love for us is much greater than our love for ourselves.

Although our culture tends to view love as an emotion, the love that Jesus is referencing is a choice—an act of the will. The love of God is called *agapē* in the Greek, and can be defined as "the steady intention of one's will toward another's highest good."[7] Jesus loves us so magnanimously that he willingly allowed his persecutors to savagely beat him and kill him by hanging him on a cross; he did this so that we might find salvation through him. There is truly no greater love than this love Jesus showed for us, in spite of our selfishness and pride. We should follow his example of love in our interaction with all people, even with those who have wronged us.

"So whatever you wish that others would do to you, do also to them, for this is the Law and the Prophets." (Matthew 7:12)

The Golden Rule. If we all lived by this, there would be neither strife nor discord; we would all live in perfect peace and harmony as Jesus would have us do.

⁂

"You shall love the Lord your God with all your heart and with all your soul and with all your mind. This is the great and first commandment. And a second is like it: You shall love your neighbor as yourself." (Matthew 22:37–39)

The Greatest Commandment. Loving God is covered by the first four of the Ten Commandments, and loving neighbor is found in the last six (see Exodus 20:3–17). Or as Paul says in Romans 13:9–10: "For the commandments, 'You shall not commit adultery, You shall not murder, You shall not steal, You shall not covet,' and any other commandment, are summed up in this word: 'You shall love your neighbor as yourself.' Love does no wrong to a neighbor; therefore love is the fulfilling of the law."

⁂

"Love your enemies and pray for those who persecute you, so that you may be sons of your Father who is in heaven." (Matthew 5:44–45)

The word Jesus uses for "love" in this passage is, again, *agapē* and can be described as benevolence. It is this goodwill which we are to bestow even on our enemies. It is impossible to love the conduct of people who bring injury or malice toward us or others, but though we may hate their conduct or even suffer from it, we should act benevolently toward them by returning good for evil. This is the highest imaginable rule of life and the most difficult of all commands to perform.

"You have heard that it was said, 'An eye for an eye and a tooth for a tooth.' But I say to you . . . if anyone slaps you on the right cheek, turn to him the other also." (Matthew 5:38–39)

Ancient law and tradition dictated that a transgression like a slap on the face would allow for like retribution. However, Jesus calls his followers to a higher standard. We are to make ourselves vulnerable instead of returning blow for blow. While this might seem passive, it is instead a way of seizing the initiative to demonstrate Christlike values rather than following the violent agenda set by the striker.

This is a difficult command to follow and another example of the radical nature of Jesus' teachings. His commandment to us can be summarized in one word: love. These verses in Matthew are an example of how we should live out his new commandment to love as he loves.

6

HIS TEACHINGS:
THE WALK OF THE KINGDOM

Following Jesus is not a one-time decision; it is an ongoing choice, and we should always be pursuing our own spiritual growth by the help of his grace. As we become more Christlike in our daily walk, we should be mindful that it is all too easy to revert to the "ways of the world." As Peter states: "Take care that you are not carried away with the error of lawless people and lose your own stability. But grow in the grace and knowledge of our Lord and Savior Jesus Christ. To him be the glory both now and to the day of eternity" (2 Peter 3:17–18).

~

FOLLOWING JESUS

To be a follower of Jesus is to walk with him, speak with him, imitate him, and pursue him in every aspect of our daily activities.

***

"Follow me." (Mark 2:14)

Jesus calls Levi, a tax collector (an outcast to the Jews), to become one of the disciples. Levi does just that, and we know him as Matthew, writer of the first Gospel. Jesus similarly invited his other disciples to follow him.

***

"Enter by the narrow gate. For the gate is wide and the way is easy that leads to destruction, and those who enter by it are many. For the gate is narrow and the way is hard that leads to life, and those who find it are few." (Matthew 7:13–14)

It is easier and more tempting to follow the examples of society—with its lusts, greed, vanity, and selfishness—than to follow Jesus. The former leads to hell (separation from God), the latter to heaven.

***

"Everyone then who hears these words of mine and does them will be like a wise man who built his house on the rock. And the rain fell, and the floods came, and the winds blew and beat on that house, but it did not fall, because it had been founded on the rock." (Matthew 7:24–25)

Jesus and his words are the only sure foundation of the soul. As we build on that foundation, our souls will know stability and will not be overwhelmed by people or spiritual forces of evil.

❈

"Whoever has my commandments and keeps them, he it is who loves me. And he who loves me will be loved by my Father, and I will love him and manifest myself to him." (John 14:21)

Jesus calls us to live a life of trust and obedience to him. James 2:26 says it succinctly: "Faith apart from works is dead." In other words, our faith is demonstrated by what we do. This passage in John also demonstrates that the love of the Father and the love of the Son cannot be separated.

❈

"The harvest is plentiful, but the laborers are few; therefore pray earnestly to the Lord of the harvest to send out laborers into his harvest." (Matthew 9:37–38)

As Jesus walked through the villages, he saw the dispirited people (like sheep without a shepherd) and lamented that many needed to be delivered. However, apart from him and his few disciples, there were not enough people to carry the good news of Jesus to all who needed it. This would change after his resurrection, as the gospel about Jesus would spread throughout the world.

⁂

"Whoever loves father or mother more than me is not worthy of me, and whoever loves son or daughter more than me is not worthy of me. And whoever does not take his cross and follow me is not worthy of me. Whoever finds his life will lose it, and whoever loses his life for my sake will find it." (Matthew 10:37–39)

Jesus requires us to make him our greatest priority. Missionary Jim Elliot brilliantly captured the essence of this text: "He is no fool who gives what he cannot keep to gain that which he cannot lose."[8] After penning these words, Elliot was murdered by the people in Ecuador he was trying to evangelize. He gave his life to be a disciple of Jesus.

⁂

"Come to me, all who labor and are heavy laden, and I will give you rest. Take my yoke upon you, and learn from me, for I am gentle and lowly in heart, and you will find rest for your souls. For my yoke is easy, and my burden is light." (Matthew 11:28–30)

These verses are first a call to trust in Jesus—to enter into the rest he offers in a personal relationship with him. Secondly, this passage is a call to follow (and keep following) Jesus as a committed disciple, relying on him for daily strength. Following Jesus is more than a religion or keeping a set of rules. It's a new life marked by peace and rest in him.

※

"Truly, I say to you, unless you turn and become like children, you will never enter the kingdom of heaven." (Matthew 18:3)

Since little children typically lack ambition, pride, and haughtiness, they are humble and teachable, the characteristics that Jesus requires of his disciples. We must set aside our selfish ambitions and pride, becoming childlike as we grip the Father's hand. Hebrews 11:6 describes this trusting faith: "Without faith it is impossible to please [God], for whoever would draw near to God must believe that he exists and that he rewards those who seek him."

※

"Do not be anxious about tomorrow, for tomorrow will be anxious for itself. Sufficient for the day is its own trouble." (Matthew 6:34)

Jesus is saying that today is all we have—we cannot return to the past, and we are not guaranteed the future. By living in the present tense during our earthly sojourn, we walk with wisdom in light of each day's opportunity.

❦

"Truly, truly, I say to you, whoever hears my word and believes him who sent me has eternal life. He does not come into judgment, but has passed from death to life." (John 5:24)

Jesus promises three things to those who hear his word and trust in the Father: (1) They possess eternal life beginning now; (2) they will not be condemned by God; and (3) they have passed from a sphere of death into the kingdom of life. The belief Jesus is speaking about is not referring to a belief *about* him (as in a proposition) but to a belief *in* him (as a person).

∼

PURSUING GOD FIRST

The following passages emphasize that we should practice certain disciplines (e.g., fasting, praying, giving to the poor, practicing righteousness) and generally live our lives for an audience of one, namely God. We should not perform good deeds to impress other people, because if we do, then the approval we receive from them will be our only reward. Instead, we should strive to please God first and find the true reward that comes from obedience to him.

�֎

"But seek first the kingdom of God and his righteousness, and all these things will be added to you." (Matthew 6:33)

Jesus is telling us to seek God above all else and that, when we do, God will provide all that we need. Thus, we need not be anxious for anything.

✖

"Beware of practicing your righteousness before other people in order to be seen by them, for then you will have no reward from your Father who is in heaven." (Matthew 6:1)

In our lives, we should seek the praise and approval of God alone, which brings eternal reward, rather than the applause and accolades of people. This applies to any of our good deeds—whether acts of kindness toward a stranger, financial giving to church, volunteering for community service, etc.

✖

"When you give to the needy, do not let your left hand know what your right hand is doing, so that your giving may be in secret. And your Father who sees in secret will reward you." (Matthew 6:3–4)

Again, calling attention to ourselves when we do good for others "spoils" those actions. Instead, Jesus commands us to play to an audience of One—trusting that God "rewards those who seek him" (Hebrews 11:6).

⁂

"When you pray, go into your room and shut the door and pray to your Father who is in secret. And your Father who sees in secret will reward you." (Matthew 6:6)

The principle that applies to giving applies to our prayers, which should be offered not to impress people but to commune with God. This verse does not discourage praying with others but speaks to our need to focus attention on him rather than an audience of others.

⁂

"When you fast, anoint your head and wash your face, that your fasting may not be seen by others but by your Father who is in secret. And your Father who sees in secret will reward you." (Matthew 6:17–18)

We don't hear much about the discipline of fasting in our churches or among followers of Jesus today. Although we have learned from modern research that fasting provides some health benefits, a true fast does not call attention to ourselves but focuses our attention on God.

$\sim$

PRACTICING HUMILITY

Humility refers to a right understanding of ourselves in relation to both our sinfulness and God's grace. The biblical doctrine of grace humbles us without degrading us and elevates us without inflating us. Thus, true humility is the realization that everything we have (health, prosperity, intellect, heritage, etc.) has been given to us.

"Everyone who exalts himself will be humbled, and he who humbles himself will be exalted." (Luke 14:11)

This verse is a warning to those who boast and see themselves as better than others. But those who are humble will be honored in the presence of God. As it's been said, "Humility is not thinking less of yourself; it is thinking of yourself less."[9]

"Whoever would be great among you must be your servant, and whoever would be first among you must be your slave, even as the Son of Man came not to be served but to serve, and to give his life as a ransom for many." (Matthew 20:26–28)

Just as Jesus humbled himself for our salvation, a humble spirit is the way of the kingdom of God. To demonstrate this spirit, Jesus serves his disciples by washing their feet.

※

"If anyone would be first, he must be last of all and servant of all." (Mark 9:35)

This verse captures the essence of servant leadership; our focus should be serving others and putting others' needs above our own, as Jesus consistently did.

～

LIVING AS STEWARDS

God is the maker and giver of all things, and we are on earth as his stewards. As stewards, we possess nothing but are managing the possessions that God has entrusted to us. Viewing material wealth and goods this way will help prevent them from becoming a snare to us in our walk with God.

※

"This poor widow has put in more than all those who are contributing to the offering box. For they all contributed out of their abundance, but she out of her poverty has put in everything she had, all she had to live on." (Mark 12:43–44)

Jesus comments on the action of a poor widow who gives only one mite (a small coin, like a penny) as her offering, because it was a large portion of what she owned. Her giving is proportionately greater than that of the rich who gave only a small portion of their wealth.

⚘

"Lay up for yourselves treasures in heaven, where neither moth nor rust destroys and where thieves do not break in and steal. For where your treasure is, there your heart will be also." (Matthew 6:20–21)

Our hearts are naturally designed to pursue profit (treasure). Thus, it is important that our definition of profit is the same as God's. We should not spend all our efforts on worldly pursuits, but our chief concern should be the things that endure. To pursue and ultimately find treasure in heaven—where nothing corrupts and no enemies plunder or destroy—would be our wisest investment on this earth. As C. S. Lewis writes in *Mere Christianity*, "Aim at Heaven and you will get earth 'thrown in': aim at earth and you will get neither."[10]

⚘

"No one can serve two masters, for either he will hate the one and love the other, or he will be devoted to the one and despise the other. You cannot serve God and money." (Matthew 6:24)

We cannot play by two sets of rules, or we will become double-minded. Either the principles of God or the principles of the world will guide us. If we are playing by the world's standards, it will be natural to accumulate and hoard earthly wealth for ourselves. Instead, Jesus commands us to hold the resources of this world with a loose grip, and to treasure the unseen (the eternal) over the seen (the temporal). He is not telling us that it is wrong to excel in the temporal arena, but this must never be the primary purpose for our endeavors.

⚜

"Truly, I say to you, only with difficulty will a rich person enter the kingdom of heaven. Again I tell you, it is easier for a camel to go through the eye of a needle than for a rich person to enter the kingdom of God." (Matthew 19:23–24)

The hyperbole here is palpable, but Jesus is emphasizing the point that if we focus entirely on pursuing and accumulating wealth to the detriment of pursuing him and a godly life, those riches will become an idol. The point is that as we become rich and successful, we tend to believe that our achievements are entirely our own doing rather than what they truly are—a gift of God.

⚜

"Take care, and be on your guard against all covetousness." (Luke 12:15)

Greed is a form of coveting and a violation of the tenth commandment (Exodus 20:17). Clearly, we need to be alert to avoid such transgression. This is even more difficult today in our consumer-driven society.

⁂

"Everyone to whom much was given, of him much will be required, and from him to whom they entrusted much, they will demand the more." (Luke 12:48)

This verse is an important challenge to all who have been blessed materially (*treasure*). Those who have been given success and wealth are expected to share with those in need. Likewise, those who have been blessed with the *talent* to teach are to use that skill to bring the knowledge of Jesus to others. And those blessed with spare *time* are to use it wisely and not only for their own entertainment.

⁂

"One who is faithful in a very little is also faithful in much, and one who is dishonest in a very little is also dishonest in much. If then you have not been faithful in the unrighteous wealth, who will entrust to you the true riches? And if you have not been faithful in that which is another's, who will give you that which is your own?" (Luke 16:10–12)

True wealth is only found in heaven, and that should be our heart's desire. Therefore, we must be honest in all things, small and large, for if we cheat or steal in the small things, our dishonesty will spill over in the way we handle larger matters and will affect our reward in the kingdom of heaven.

7

HIS WORDS TO HIS DISCIPLES

Jesus chose to invest his time in a small group of followers, known as the twelve disciples (or apostles), who became the recipients of some of his most important instructions. Eleven of the original disciples continued to follow him after his death and resurrection—becoming some of the first to carry his message to the world. Judas, one of the original Twelve, betrayed Jesus to the authorities, and tragically committed suicide. Another man, Matthias, was chosen to take Judas's place as the twelfth disciple.

The apostle Paul (known as Saul prior to his conversion) was not among the original Twelve, but he is later counted as an apostle, and thus Jesus' words to him are included at the end of this chapter.

Each of Jesus' original disciples—with the exception of John (who died in exile) and, of course, Judas—was martyred for preaching the gospel. This fact is offered as one of many historical evidences of the truth of the resurrection. Certainly, no one would go to their death preaching something they did not fervently believe.

Some of the passages that follow detail events prior to Jesus' crucifixion, such as his recruitment of the disciples and an event known as the transfiguration. Other messages came after his death and resurrection, most prominently the Great Commission, which he gave to his disciples before he ascended to the Father.

✠

"Follow me, and I will make you fishers of men." (Matthew 4:19)

Jesus' first recruits are ordinary, uneducated fishermen. In the future they will "catch" believers in Christ, not fish. Upon hearing his voice, they (Peter, Andrew, John, and James) drop their nets and follow him. They would be with him to the end of his earthly life.

✠

"Do not fear those who kill the body but cannot kill the soul. Rather fear him who can destroy both soul and body in hell." (Matthew 10:28)

People may threaten us on this earth; some may even be in a position to destroy our earthly bodies. It's natural to be fearful of this, but we can replace this fear with faith when we have the assurance of being with him in eternity.

※

"Blessed are you, Simon Bar-Jonah! For flesh and blood has not revealed this to you, but my Father who is in heaven. And I tell you, you are Peter, and on this rock I will build my church, and the gates of hell shall not prevail against it." (Matthew 16:17–18)

After Jesus asks, "Who do you say that I am?" (v. 15), Peter answers, "You are the Christ, the Son of the living God" (v. 16). Note that Jesus changes Simon's name to Peter or Petra (which means "rock"); and indeed, Peter's confession would be the foundation upon which the church would be built and extended throughout the world. It is through the church that God overcomes the opposition of the enemy.

※

"If anyone would come after me, let him deny himself and take up his cross and follow me. For whoever would save his life will lose it, but whoever loses his life for my sake will find it." (Matthew 16:24–25)

The time we spend here on this earth is miniscule compared to what awaits in heaven. As Paul says, "I consider that the sufferings of this present time are not worth comparing with the glory that is to be revealed to us" (Romans 8:18). In other words, rather than giving our lives for temporary goods, we should exchange them for eternal treasure.

❧

"Rise, and have no fear." (Matthew 17:7)

In an event called "the transfiguration," Jesus' appearance is transformed in the presence of three of his disciples. His face shines like the sun, his clothes become white like light, and he speaks with Moses and Elijah (two significant Old Testament prophets), who also appear. A voice out of the cloud says, "This is my beloved Son, with whom I am well pleased; listen to him" (v. 5). (You'll recall that similar words were heard as Jesus came out of the water at his baptism.) To witness this scene and hear the voice of God was a defining moment in the lives of Peter, James, and John.

❧

"If you abide in my word, you are truly my disciples, and you will know the truth, and the truth will set you free." (John 8:31–32)

The truth that Jesus speaks of is not merely a proposition to be believed but a person (Jesus) to be received and trusted. He is the only one who can set us free from the bondage that sin produces. Our obedience to him becomes an expression of our commitment to his truth.

※

"And whatever you ask in prayer, you will receive, if you have faith." (Matthew 21:22)

This verse would seem to imply that we will receive everything we ask from God; however, only he knows what is best for us and those for whom we pray. What we think of as favorable for ourselves or others may not be so in the mind of God. However, he only desires what is best for us in the long run. This is not an easy concept, particularly in those situations where we pray for the healing of others; only by faith in God can we endure when our prayers are not answered as we wish.

※

"Take, eat; this is my body. . . . Drink of [this cup], all of you, for this is my blood of the covenant, which is poured out for many for the forgiveness of sins." (Matthew 26:26–28)

Jesus speaks these words at the Last Supper, a meal he ate with his disciples shortly before he was betrayed, arrested, and killed. These are also the words usually spoken during Holy Communion (sometimes called the Lord's Supper or the Eucharist) during Christian services. In this celebration, we remember Christ's sacrifice for us. His shed blood gives us hope after death.

❧

"No longer do I call you servants. . . . I have called you friends, for all that I have heard from my Father I have made known to you. You did not choose me, but I chose you and appointed you that you should go and bear fruit . . . so that whatever you ask the Father in my name, he may give it to you. These things I command you, so that you will love one other." (John 15:15–17)

These are some of Jesus' final instructions to his disciples. He has taught them and expects them to go forward and spread his teachings. Thus he tells them that he picked them for this purpose and that God will be with them in the future. He also commands them to love each other, and he commands us to do likewise.

❧

"In my Father's house are many rooms. If it were not so, would I have told you that I go to prepare a place for you? And if I go and prepare a place for you, I will come again and will take you to myself, that where I am you may be also." (John 14:2–3)

This promise of Jesus is an allusion to the Jewish custom of a bridegroom—having prepared a special place for his bride in his father's house—coming to bring his bride there for the marriage ceremony. Likewise, Jesus is promising to take his followers to join him in the Father's house.

⁂

"Go therefore and make disciples of all nations, baptizing them in the name of the Father and of the Son and of the Holy Spirit, teaching them to observe all that I have commanded you." (Matthew 28:19–20)

The Great Commission. Jesus instructs his disciples to make other disciples and spread the knowledge of God to the entire world. His words apply not only to the disciples he originally commissioned, but to us as well. It is our call and opportunity to follow that same guidance in whatever context he has placed us. True disciples do not separate their spiritual world from their secular world, but in all things demonstrate how to live before God: "Live and speak in such a way that those who know you, but don't know God, will come to know God because they know and have observed you."[11]

⁂

"Behold, I am with you always, to the end of the age." (Matthew 28:20)

Jesus makes this comforting and empowering promise to all of his followers: He is there for us in both the good times and in our deepest, darkest moments.

⁂

"I will ask the Father, and he will give you another Helper [the Holy Spirit], to be with you forever." (John 14:16)

"[Jesus] ordered [the apostles] . . . to wait for the promise of the Father, which, he said, 'you heard from me; for John baptized with water, but you will be baptized with the Holy Spirit not many days from now.'" (Acts 1:4–5)

Jesus explains to his disciples that the Holy Spirit will soon be among them and will indwell and empower them to spread the gospel. Fifty days after the resurrection, the disciples are celebrating the Jewish day of Pentecost when the Holy Spirit comes upon them. Immediately, they begin speaking the wonders of God to foreign strangers in the tongue of each one, although none of them knew the languages that they were speaking (Acts 2:1–12). This event marks the birth of the Church, as Jesus' disciples go forth in the power of the Spirit to spread the good news about him.

⁂

"Saul, Saul, why are you persecuting me? . . . I am Jesus. . . . But rise and enter the city, and you will be told what you are to do." (Acts 9:4–6)

Saul, who was persecuting the "Jesus followers," is struck blind and spoken to by the resurrected Jesus. After this experience, he becomes Paul, known as the Apostle to the Gentiles (apostle means "sent one"). A zealous follower of Christ, he spreads the good news of Jesus throughout the Roman Empire and also becomes the author of the greatest number of books in the New Testament.

※

"Go, for he is a chosen instrument of mine to carry my name before the Gentiles and kings and the children of Israel. For I will show him how much he must suffer for the sake of my name." (Acts 9:15–16)

Jesus speaks to Ananias (a follower of Jesus) about the impact Saul (later Paul) will make as well as the price of adversity he will pay to spread the gospel. Paul will be whipped, beaten, stoned, threatened with death, shipwrecked three times, bitten by a deadly serpent, left starving in the cold without adequate clothing, and imprisoned—all because of his belief and teaching about Christ. And he will never waver in that belief, all the way up until his death (tradition tells us that he was beheaded under the Roman Emperor Nero).

8

HIS PRAYERS

Jesus prayed often with his disciples and also took time to be alone praying to his heavenly Father. Each of us should follow his example of both private and corporate (group) fellowship with God. Following are some important prayers of Jesus. The first one—known as "the Lord's Prayer"—is a God-given template for how we should pray.

✿

"Our Father in heaven, hallowed be your name. Your kingdom come, your will be done, on earth as it is in heaven. Give us this day our daily bread, and forgive us our debts, as we also have forgiven our debtors. And lead us not into temptation, but deliver us from evil." (Matthew 6:9–13)

The Lord's Prayer. Jesus gives us an example of how we should pray: praising God first, thanking him for all blessings, asking him for forgiveness of our sins, and asking for protection in times of temptation and spiritual adversity. Note that unlike most of our own prayers, this prayer submits to God's larger purposes for our lives that we may not understand. It has been said that God is not a cosmic vending machine, dispensing what we seek for our own benefit; we may know what we want, but he knows what is really best for us, and it always ends up— in the long run—being better than what we asked for.

※

"Father, I thank you that you have heard me. I knew that you always hear me, but I said this on account of the people standing around, that they may believe that you sent me." (John 11:41–42)

Jesus is publicly acknowledging the Father as he raises Lazarus from the dead. He took days to arrive at the gravesite to make sure that everyone knew Lazarus had been dead and buried for three days. Thus, when he is raised up on the fourth day, it is clear through this sign that Jesus has come forth from God.

※

"Father, the hour has come; glorify your Son that the Son may glorify you . . . with the glory that I had with you before the world existed." (John 17:1, 5)

On the night of his betrayal, Jesus prays to the Father, knowing that he would be arrested that night and crucified the next day. As the God-man, he refers to the glory he enjoyed with the Father before all time. (As we noted before, Jesus' presence before the creation is inferred in Genesis 1:26 when God uses the plural pronoun "our" to refer to himself.)

⁕

"I do not ask for these [the twelve apostles] only, but also for those who will believe in me through their word, that they may all be one, just as you, Father, are in me, and I in you, that they also may be in us, so that the world may believe that you have sent me. The glory that you have given me I have given to them, that they may be one even as we are one, I in them and you in me, that they may become perfectly one, so that the world may know that you sent me and loved them even as you loved me." (John 17:20–23)

Just before he is betrayed, Jesus prays not only for his disciples but also for all who would believe through them.

⁕

"My Father, if it be possible, let this cup pass from me; nevertheless, not as I will, but as you will." (Matthew 26:39)

As Jesus is praying in the Garden of Gethsemane (where he will be betrayed), he anticipates the anguish to come. The cup to which he refers is more than the gruesomeness of a Roman crucifixion; it is separation from the Father when he bears the sins of the world. He asks the Father if there is another way to accomplish this without going to the cross. Yet he accepts the purpose for which he came in obedience to the Father's will.

9

HIS OPPOSITION

Jesus has numerous confrontations with his adversaries and always responds in an ingenious or witty manner, often quoting Scripture. His first significant opposition on record is with the devil himself, but more often he is questioned or challenged by the Jewish leaders, many of whom feel threatened by him, his teachings, his actions, and the Jewish people's attraction to him. These leaders, most prominently the Pharisees (the most influential Jewish sect), cannot accept that he is the Messiah prophesied by the Old Testament; to do so would be a grave threat to their power and influence. Jesus challenges them openly about their corruption and their legalistic system. He also faces the Roman authorities, specifically the governor of Judea, Pontius Pilate, who ultimately condemns him to death.

"It is written, 'Man shall not live by bread alone, but by every word that comes from the mouth of God.' . . . Again it is written, 'You shall not put the Lord your God to the test.' . . . Be gone, Satan! For it is written, 'You shall worship the Lord your God and him only shall you serve.'" (Matthew 4:4, 7, 10)

After Jesus fasts for forty days and nights, he is confronted by Satan. Satan tries to tempt him first by offering him food when he is famished, then by challenging him to display his power, then by offering him the authority and splendor of the kingdoms of the earth. These temptations reflect the three categories in which all people are tempted—"the desires of the flesh and the desires of the eyes and pride of life" (1 John 2:16). In each temptation, Jesus uses Scripture to refute the devil, who departs after the third temptation.

※

"The Son of Man is lord even of the Sabbath." (Mark 2:28)

This is Jesus' response after the Pharisees accuse him of working on the Sabbath. His response is that, as the Son of Man, he has authority over the Sabbath.

※

"Is it lawful on the Sabbath to do good or to do harm, to save life or to kill?" (Mark 3:4)

Jesus is demonstrating how legalistic the Pharisees' approach to the law has become. He further points out that if they had a sheep that fell into a pit on a Sabbath, they would certainly lift it out, even though, by their own definition, that action would be considered breaking the Sabbath. After saying these words, Jesus heals a man's withered hand in the synagogue. Immediately, the Pharisees begin to plot how to kill him.

⁂

"A prophet is not without honor, except in his hometown . . . and in his own household." (Mark 6:4)

Even at the inception of his ministry, when he returns to his hometown of Nazareth, although he has been performing many miracles in the area, those who knew him from childhood do not take him seriously. They cannot move beyond their perception of him as the son of a carpenter named Joseph. Consequently, they cannot accept him as the Messiah.

⁂

"Those who are well have no need of a physician, but those who are sick. I have not come to call the righteous but sinners to repentance." (Luke 5:31–32)

This is Jesus' answer to the Pharisees when they question why he spends time with "sinners." Because of their rule keeping, the Pharisees suppose themselves to be righteous. In reality, no one (except Jesus) is without sin.

※

"Is it not written, 'My house shall be called a house of prayer for all the nations'? But you have made it a den of robbers." (Mark 11:17)

Jesus rebukes the peddlers and money changers who are transacting their business within the temple, thereby dishonoring the house of God. Consequently, the chief priests and other Jewish teachers begin to plot to kill him as they fear him and his teachings.

※

"Woe to you lawyers also! For you load people with burdens hard to bear, and you yourselves do not touch the burdens with one of your fingers. Woe to you! For you build the tombs of the prophets whom your fathers killed." (Luke 11:46–47)

Again, Jesus calls out the Jewish leaders for their hypocrisy. Rather than serving the people as they should, they oppressed them with traditions that they had invented and added to the law of God.

❁

"You are those who justify yourselves before men, but God knows your hearts. For what is exalted among men is an abomination in the sight of God." (Luke 16:15)

With these words, Jesus directly challenges the Pharisees, whom he decries as sanctimonious in their practice. These leaders were demanding strict observance of external forms and ceremonies of religion and conduct, without regard for the true spirit of God's law, which was about loving God and others.

❁

"Why put me to the test, you hypocrites? Show me the coin for the tax. . . . Render to Caesar the things that are Caesar's, and to God the things that are God's." (Matthew 22:18–19, 21)

This is Jesus' shrewd answer to the Pharisees when they try to trap him by asking him if a person should pay the imperial tax to the Roman government. An answer of *no* would have been considered treason by the Romans; an answer of *yes* would have been considered anti-nationalist by the Jewish people. Caesar's image is on the coin that is shown. Jesus is using the coin to illustrate the distinction between the human and divine spheres of authority.

"Woe to you, scribes and Pharisees, hypocrites! For you . . . have neglected the weightier matters of the law: justice and mercy and faithfulness. . . . You are like whitewashed tombs, which outwardly appear beautiful, but within are full of dead people's bones and all uncleanness. So you also outwardly appear righteous to others, but within you are full of hypocrisy and lawlessness." (Matthew 23:23, 27–28)

Jesus directly challenges the Pharisees as they hold themselves up as the leaders and guardians of the laws of the Old Testament. They have become legalistic and pompous, separating themselves from the people and holding themselves up as righteous. Yet, in truth, they are hypocrites—their righteousness was an outward appearance but not an inward reality.

"I am, and you will see the Son of Man seated at the right hand of Power, and coming with the clouds of heaven." (Mark 14:62)

This is Jesus' response to the question of the high priest: "Are you the Christ, the Son of the Blessed?" (v. 61). Upon Jesus' affirmative answer to being the Messiah, the high priest tears his clothes and says, "You have heard his blasphemy" (v. 64), and the Jewish leaders all condemn him as worthy of death. In making this claim to the Jewish leaders, Jesus knows he is issuing his own death sentence.

※

"You say that I am a king. For this purpose I was born and for this purpose I have come into the world—to bear witness to the truth. Everyone who is of the truth listens to my voice." (John 18:37)

This is Jesus' answer to Pontius Pilate's question, "You are a king?" God is truth, and Jesus came into the world as the incarnate truth and the way to the Father. As he says in John 14:6, "I am the way, and the truth, and the life."

※

"My kingdom is not of this world. If my kingdom were of this world, my servants would have been fighting, that I might not be delivered over to the Jews. But my kingdom is not from the world." (John 18:36)

"You would have no authority over me at all unless it had been given you from above." (John 19:11)

In the same conversation with Pontius Pilate just cited, Jesus asserts his origin (heaven) and his deity, implying that if he desired, he could strike down Pilate and his legions. Jesus is not a helpless victim but a willing sacrifice. He is allowing himself to be tortured and killed, although he has the power to prevent these things. He does so to fulfill the purpose for which the Father sent him to earth.

10

HIS DEATH AND RESURRECTION

Jesus foretold his betrayal, death by crucifixion, and resurrection on the third day. Because he knew that he had come to fulfill the prophecies concerning the Messiah, he became a willing substitute for the sins of his people as predicted of the Suffering Servant in Isaiah 53:3–11.

The resurrection of Jesus is the central historical event in the Christian faith. As the apostle Paul put it, "If Christ has not been raised, then our preaching is in vain and your faith is in vain" (1 Corinthians 15:14).

"Destroy this temple, and in three days I will raise it up." (John 2:19)

Whereas the Jews think Jesus is speaking of the Jewish temple in Jerusalem and therefore laugh at these words, Jesus is actually speaking metaphorically of his physical body—which will be crucified and then raised from the dead on the third day.

※

"For just as Jonah was three days and three nights in the belly of the great fish, so will the Son of Man be three days and three nights in the heart of the earth." (Matthew 12:40)

Jesus uses the analogy of the prophet Jonah as a sign of his own death, burial, and resurrection.

※

"For this reason the Father loves me, because I lay down my life that I may take it up again. No one takes it from me, but I lay it down of my own accord. I have authority to lay it down, and I have authority to take it up again." (John 10:17–18)

Unlike the sacrificial animals mandated by the Old Testament law, Jesus willingly gave himself in obedience to the Father's purpose to pay for the sins of the world. The apostle Paul describes the importance of Christ's sacrifice in this way: "For our sake [God] made him to be sin who knew no sin, so that in him we might become the righteousness of God" (2 Corinthians 5:21).

※

"The Son of Man is about to be delivered into the hands of men, and they will kill him, and he will be raised on the third day." (Matthew 17:22–23)

Jesus describes in advance what will actually occur: He will be betrayed, captured, interrogated, tortured, crucified, and buried. Then he will rise again on the third day.

�֍֎

"The Son of Man will be delivered over to the chief priests and scribes, and they will condemn him to death and deliver him over to the Gentiles to be mocked and flogged and crucified, and he will be raised on the third day." (Matthew 20:18–19)

While traveling to Jerusalem, Jesus prepares his disciples for what will be taking place after they enter the city. These events occur just as he foretold.

✖

"The hour has come for the Son of Man to be glorified. Truly, truly, I say to you, unless a grain of wheat falls into the earth and dies, it remains alone; but if it dies, it bears much fruit." (John 12:23–24)

Jesus is speaking of his death and resurrection, comparing his death to that of the seed of a plant, which must die so that other plants can grow.

✖

"A little while, and you will see me no longer; and again a little while, and you will see me. . . . You have sorrow now, but I will see you again, and your hearts will rejoice, and no one will take your joy from you." (John 16:16, 22)

Jesus is preparing his disciples for the awful separation that will take place as a result of his death. Their sorrow will turn to joy when they see him again in his resurrected body.

⚜

"Behold, the hour is coming, indeed it has come, when you will be scattered, each to his own home, and will leave me alone. Yet I am not alone, for the Father is with me. I have said these things to you, that in me you may have peace. In the world you will have tribulation. But take heart; I have overcome the world." (John 16:32–33)

Jesus accurately predicts that all of his disciples will desert him at the time of his capture. Though they will encounter adversity from the world, they will walk in his peace as his followers because he has overcome sin and death and has given them eternal life.

⚜

"The Son of Man goes as it is written of him, but woe to that man by whom the Son of Man is betrayed! It would have been better for that man if he had not been born." (Matthew 26:24)

As the messianic prophecies predicted, Jesus will be betrayed by one of his own. He laments that his betrayer, Judas, will suffer a miserable death (which he does by hanging himself—see Matthew 27:5). Ever since this event, the name Judas has been used to connote a betrayer.

❦

"'Eli, Eli, lema sabachthani?' that is, 'My God, my God, why have you forsaken me?'" (Matthew 27:46)

In some of his final words on the cross, Jesus quotes Psalm 22, speaking of the awful separation from the Father that he will experience on behalf of his people as he takes upon himself the sins of the world.

❦

"It is finished." (John 19:30)

"Father, into your hands I commit my spirit!" (Luke 23:46)

These final words of Jesus on the cross signify the fulfillment of his purpose in coming to earth—to bear the sins of the world. Having completed his work, he is able to return to the Father.

❦

"Woman, why are you weeping? Whom are you seeking?" (John 20:15)

On the third day after Jesus was crucified, Mary Magdalene visits the tomb where Jesus was buried and finds it empty. She begins sobbing and saying, "They have taken away my Lord" (v. 13). She is astonished to see the risen Jesus, who speaks to her. Immediately, she joyfully runs to tell the others of the miracle of his resurrection.

⁂

"Put your finger here, and see my hands; and put out your hand, and place it in my side. Do not disbelieve, but believe. . . . Have you believed because you have seen me? Blessed are those who have not seen and yet have believed." (John 20:27, 29)

Jesus appeared to the other disciples in the absence of Thomas, and when the others explain to him what happened, he refuses to believe that Jesus has risen. He is only convinced when Jesus suddenly appears in his presence and implores him to touch his wounds (hence the term "doubting Thomas").

⁂

"Peace be with you. As the Father has sent me, even so I am sending you." (John 20:21)

Jesus, in his resurrected body, miraculously appears in a locked room to the disciples the evening after he rose from the dead. He commissions them and sends them out into the world in his peace and power.

11

HIS OFFER OF SALVATION

We have a major decision in life: to pursue life with God or to pursue a life apart from him. There is no third choice. The consequences of the wrong choice are more than any of us would be willing to face if we really understood them. Unfortunately, many people move through life without grasping those consequences. We may think that being a "good person" is adequate for our salvation but fail to use the right measuring stick—comparing ourselves to other people instead of to God's perfect standard. His standard is the only one that matters in the end, and no person except Jesus is able to attain it (Romans 3:23). As a result, trusting in Jesus is our only hope. Paul tells us in Romans 10:9–10: "If you confess with your mouth that Jesus is Lord and believe in your heart that God raised him from the dead, you will be saved. For with the heart one believes and is justified, and with the mouth one confesses and is saved."

The great French theologian and mathematician Blaise Pascal presented a "wager" to show that a rational person should live as though God exists and seek to believe in God. On the one hand, if God does not actually exist, a person who believes in him will suffer a finite loss—some pleasures, riches, and the like—while standing to receive infinite gains (eternity with God). On the other hand, if God does exist, believing in him will avoid infinite losses (eternity apart from God). Indeed, in this case, not to choose heaven is by default to choose hell, as there is no middle ground.[12]

The verses in this chapter emphasize the choice we all make and the future prospects of those who choose eternal life with God. These verses also emphasize that belief in the Lord Jesus is essential to salvation. This belief is not simply knowledge of Jesus as an historical figure or "just another" moral or spiritual leader, but a personal trust in him. This belief prompts a conviction to follow his teachings and to seek forgiveness when we fail to live up to his example.

"For God so loved the world, that he gave his only Son, that whoever believes in him should not perish but have eternal life." (John 3:16)

This is the essence of the gospel. What it means to believe in Jesus is amplified in the prologue to John's Gospel: "He came to his own, and his own people did not receive him. But to all who did receive him, who believed in his name, he gave the right to become children of God" (1:11–12). This passage teaches that believing in Jesus is not merely an intellectual decision but a personal reception that transforms people into the spiritual children of God whose eternal life now dwells in them.

⁂

"I am the resurrection and the life. Whoever believes in me, though he die, yet shall he live, and everyone who lives and believes in me shall never die." (John 11:25–26)

Because Jesus rose from the dead, all those who trust in him will also rise from the dead.

⁂

"For this is the will of my Father, that everyone who looks on the Son and believes in him should have eternal life, and I will raise him up on the last day." (John 6:40)

Jesus' offer of eternal life is made to all who entrust themselves to him.

⁂

"If anyone would come after me, let him deny himself and take up his cross and follow me. For whoever would save his life will lose it, but whoever loses his life for my sake and the gospel's will save it." (Mark 8:34–35)

Although salvation is a free gift, discipleship (following Jesus) has a high cost. To "take up our cross" means to submit and surrender ourselves to God's purposes, which may entail adversities we would never seek on our own.

❧

"Truly, truly, I say to you, if anyone keeps my word, he will never see death." (John 8:51)

The new life Jesus offers is spiritual rather than biological.

❧

"Truly, truly, I say to you, whoever receives the one I send receives me, and whoever receives me receives the one who sent me." (John 13:20)

To receive Jesus is to receive the Father.

❧

"So everyone who acknowledges me before men, I also will acknowledge before my Father who is in heaven, but whoever denies me before men, I also will deny before my Father who is in heaven." (Matthew 10:32–33)

"Whoever is ashamed of me and of my words in this adulterous and sinful generation, of him will the Son of Man also be ashamed when he comes in the glory of his Father with the holy angels." (Mark 8:38)

To possess eternal life in Jesus means we will be willing to take the risk of professing him before others. If we are ashamed to confess that we are his followers, then it's justifiable to question whether we have really come to know him.

✿

"Ask, and it will be given to you; seek, and you will find; knock, and it will be opened to you. For everyone who asks receives, and the one who seeks finds, and to the one who knocks it will be opened." (Matthew 7:7–8)

It's been said that there are two kinds of people in the world—those who seek to know God and those who seek to avoid him—and both will succeed in the end. All who ask, seek, and knock will come to know God.

✿

"Truly, truly, I say to you, unless one is born again he cannot see the kingdom of God." (John 3:3)

Jesus tells Nicodemus about the need for a spiritual and not merely a biological birth. All of us have received the first birth, which is physical, but only those who have received Jesus receive the second birth, which is spiritual.

"With man this is impossible, but with God all things are possible." (Matthew 19:26)

This is Jesus' response to his disciples' question, "Who then can be saved?" His reply tells us that salvation is by God's mercy. We are all sinners and do not deserve salvation, but by seeking God through Jesus we receive better than we deserve. We cannot obtain this through our own works but only by belief and trust in Jesus.

"For many are called, but few are chosen." (Matthew 22:14)

The offer of salvation is made to all, without bias or prejudice, but God has given us the capacity to respond to his initiatives. Jesus' offer is real, but we have to either receive or reject it. To ignore his offer is effectively to reject it. Because of our tendency to pursue what is seen (this world) over the unseen (eternity in heaven), it is no surprise that few choose to accept Jesus' invitation.

❧

"Truly, I say to you, today you will be with me in paradise." (Luke 23:43)

Jesus utters these words to one of the two criminals crucified beside him. That criminal, a thief, acknowledged the deity of Christ and sought forgiveness, while the other mocked him. Thus, Jesus is affirming that it is never too late to come to salvation, regardless of our sinful past. The two criminals' responses mirror our two options: accept Jesus into our lives or reject him. There is no third option.

❧

"Those who are considered worthy to attain to that age and to the resurrection from the dead . . . cannot die anymore, because they are equal to angels and are sons of God, being sons of the resurrection. . . . He is not God of the dead, but of the living, for all live to him." (Luke 20:35–36, 38)

We are not in the land of the living going to the land of the dying. Jesus gives us the opportunity to be transferred from the land of the dying to the land of the living by putting our trust in him.

12

HIS TEACHINGS ON THE END TIMES

Although many people immediately think of the book of Revelation when they hear of the end times, other parts of the Bible also speak of these events. Jesus himself spoke quite vividly of the last days on multiple occasions. He told us that he will return; that not even he knows when that will happen; that it will happen quickly, but only after great upheaval and perilous times; and that the Father has given him the authority to judge the righteous (that is, those who have been justified by faith in him) and the unrighteous.

The apostle Paul describes the coming of Christ for his own in this way: "For the Lord himself will descend from heaven with a cry of command, with the voice of an archangel, and with the sound of the trumpet of God. And the dead in Christ will rise first. Then we who are alive, who are left, will be caught up together with them in the clouds to meet the Lord in the air, and so we will always be with the Lord" (1 Thessalonians 4:16–17). If we are wise, we will live in anticipation of Jesus' summoning his beloved to the Father's house. Unlike the second coming, this event could take place at any time.

⸙

"You heard me say, 'I am going away, and I will come to you.' If you loved me, you would have rejoiced, because I am going to the Father, for the Father is greater than I. And now I have told you before it takes place, so that when it does take place you may believe." (John 14:28–29)

Jesus tells his disciples that he will be going up to heaven to be with God the Father and that he will return. At that time, Jesus will draw to himself all who have placed their trust in him.

⸙

"Beware of false prophets, who come to you in sheep's clothing but inwardly are ravenous wolves." (Matthew 7:15)

Jesus warns us that, as we approach the end, there will be false prophets. We should be on guard against these "wolves" and not allow ourselves to be deceived.

※

"And this gospel of the kingdom will be proclaimed throughout the whole world as a testimony to all nations, and then the end will come." (Matthew 24:14)

Jesus is saying that all peoples throughout the world will need to be exposed to the gospel before his second coming—a remarkable statement, given that at the time there were very few disciples, all of whom were located in one small region. Today, the gospel has for the first time reached every nation and almost all people groups.

※

"The Son of Man will send his angels, and they will gather out of his kingdom all causes of sin and all law-breakers, and throw them into the fiery furnace. In that place there will be weeping and gnashing of teeth. Then the righteous will shine like the sun in the kingdom of their Father." (Matthew 13:41–43)

"So it will be at the end of the age. The angels will come out and separate the evil from the righteous and throw them into the fiery furnace. In that place there will be weeping and gnashing of teeth." (Matthew 13:49–50)

"For as the lightning comes from the east and shines as far as the west, so will be the coming of the Son of Man. . . . Then will appear in heaven the sign of the Son of Man, and then all the tribes of the earth will mourn, and they will see the Son of Man coming on the clouds of heaven with power and great glory. And he will send out his angels with a loud trumpet call, and they will gather his elect from the four winds, from one end of heaven to the other." (Matthew 24:27, 30–31)

At his second coming, Jesus will appear suddenly without warning to judge the righteous (his elect) and the unrighteous.

HIS TEACHINGS ON THE END TIMES

"So when you see the abomination of desolation spoken of by the prophet Daniel, standing in the holy place (let the reader understand), then let those who are in Judea flee to the mountains. Let the one who is on the housetop not go down to take what is in his house, and let the one who is in the field not turn back to take his cloak. And alas for women who are pregnant and for those who are nursing infants in those days! Pray that your flight may not be in winter or on a Sabbath. For then there will be great tribulation, such as has not been from the beginning of the world until now, no, and never will be." (Matthew 24:15–21)

During a time known as the tribulation, there will be unprecedented destruction that would lead to the end of all human life if it were not cut off.

There are several views of the tribulation—a seven-year period described as the "Day of the Lord" in the Old Testament. Many scholars hold that true believers will be taken to the Father's house before the tribulation begins (this is called the rapture). Others contend that believers will endure persecution during part or all of this time. This subject is beyond the scope of this text, but in my view, the former scenario—that believers are taken up before the tribulation—is most consistent with the biblical text.[13]

"But concerning that day and hour no one knows, not even the angels of heaven, nor the Son, but the Father only.... Therefore, stay awake, for you do not know on what day your Lord is coming." (Matthew 24:36, 42)

It would be eternally unwise to postpone our reception of Jesus until it is too late. The fact that we do not know when he will return should also motivate us to walk with expectation that his return could come at any time.

❧

"But be on guard.... in those days, after that tribulation, the sun will be darkened, and the moon will not give its light, and the stars will be falling from heaven, and the powers in the heavens will be shaken. And then they will see the Son of Man coming in clouds with great power and glory." (Mark 13:23–26)

Jesus forewarns of his second coming with a quote from the Old Testament prophet Isaiah, who spoke clearly of the coming of the Messiah, describing Jesus in many ways (see Isaiah 52:13–53:12).

❧

"When the Son of Man comes in his glory . . . he will sit on his glorious throne. Before him will be gathered all the nations, and he will separate people one from another as a shepherd separates the sheep from the goats. And he will place the sheep on his right, but the goats on the left. Then the King will say to those on his right, 'Come, you who are blessed by my Father; inherit the kingdom prepared for you from the foundation of the world.' . . . Then he will say to those on his left, 'Depart from me, you cursed, into the eternal fire.'" (Matthew 25:31–34, 41)

This passage describes the judgment that will occur at the end of the tribulation period. Those who physically survive and come to faith during the tribulation will be separated from those who have rejected God. Believers will enter into the kingdom of the Lord Jesus, who will rule and reign over the earth.

※

"But I tell you, from now on you will see the Son of Man seated at the right hand of Power and coming on the clouds of heaven." (Matthew 26:64)

This is Jesus' response to the high priest when he asks if Jesus is the Christ. The "Power" is God, and the implication is that Jesus stands in judgment over the Jewish nation for its rejection of him, the Messiah.

※

"For as the Father has life in himself, so he has granted the Son also to have life in himself. And he has given him authority to execute judgment, because he is the Son of Man. Do not marvel at this, for an hour is coming when all who are in the tombs will hear his voice and come out, those who have done good to the resurrection of life, and those who have done evil to the resurrection of judgment." (John 5:26–29)

The Son of Man has been given authority to judge all people—the living and the dead, the righteous and the unrighteous.

⚜

"Heaven and earth will pass away, but my words will not pass away." (Matthew 24:35)

As Revelation 21:1 states, there will be a new heaven and a new earth, but God and his message will endure for eternity.

⚜

"It is done! I am the Alpha and the Omega, the beginning and the end. To the thirsty I will give from the spring of the water of life without payment. The one who conquers will have this heritage, and I will be his God and he will be my son. But as for the cowardly, the faithless, the detestable, as for murderers, the sexually immoral, sorcerers, idolaters, and all liars, their portion will be in the lake that burns with fire and sulfur, which is the second death." (Revelation 21:6–8)

"Behold, I am coming soon, bringing my recompense with me, to repay each one for what he has done. I am the Alpha and the Omega, the first and the last, the beginning and the end." (Revelation 22:12–13)

The awful finality of Jesus' words should drive us away from complacency to commitment to him. Our eternal destinies hang in the balance.

※

"Behold, I am making all things new." (Revelation 21:5)

Jesus promises to restore all things and defeat all death.

Scripture presents a stark contrast between the destinies of the unrighteous and the destinies of all believers. For the latter, Jesus "will wipe away every tear from their eyes, and death shall be no more, neither shall there be mourning, nor crying, nor pain anymore, for the former things have passed away" (Revelation 21:4).

CONFESSING FAITH IN JESUS

Saint Augustine wrote, "Thou hast formed us for Thyself, and our hearts are restless till they find rest in Thee."[14] In other words, we cannot find true fulfillment apart from God—and the way to God is through his Son, Jesus. Thankfully, God invites us and desires for us to seek him and promises to respond when we do so.

As we have seen, *not* to accept Jesus is effectively the same as rejecting him. To reject him is catastrophic because it is to spurn the source of life, light, and love. I invite you to seek him now by transferring your trust in your own works to his work on your behalf. You can use this simple prayer for this purpose:

Dear Lord Jesus, I know that I am a sinner, and I ask for your forgiveness. I believe you died for my sins and rose from the dead. I turn from my sins and invite You to come into my heart and life. I want to trust and follow You as my Lord and Savior. In Your Name, Amen.[15]

To receive Jesus is to receive the life of the Father and to be made alive by his Spirit. Now the real journey begins, an earthly pilgrimage in which you are being prepared for the Father's house.

CONTINUING THE JOURNEY

To encourage you in your journey and empower you to be more like Jesus, I recommend Ken Boa's *Handbook to Prayer* as a starting point. The book will take you by the hand and guide you into a satisfying, consistent, and enjoyable experience of prayer. It uniquely combines prayer and Scripture in such a way that you pray Scripture back to God. You can order this resource at handbooktoprayer.com.

Additional recommended resources include the following books.

- *The Case for Christ,* Lee Strobel

- *Mere Christianity,* C. S. Lewis

- *Knowing God,* J. I. Packer

- *The Pursuit of God,* A. W. Tozer

- *The Knowledge of the Holy,* A. W. Tozer

- *Basic Christianity,* John Stott

- *Life in the Presence of God,* Ken Boa

- *Conformed to His Image,* Ken Boa

- *How Now Shall We Live?,* Charles Colson and Nancy Pearcey

ENDNOTES

1. C. S. Lewis, *God in the Dock: Essays on Theology and Ethics* (Grand Rapids, MI: Eerdmans, 1970), 101.

2. C. S. Lewis, *Mere Christianity* (New York: HarperOne, 1980), 51–52.

3. Quoted in Kenneth Boa, *Conformed to His Image: Biblical, Practical Approaches to Spiritual Formation*, rev. ed. (Grand Rapids, MI: Zondervan, 2020), 479.

4. This quote is part of a passage (John 7:53–8:11) that is not in most of the early manuscripts of the Gospel of John. However, it's likely that the story is authentic, and it does teach principles that are in keeping with the rest of Scripture.

5. From notes on an in-person study taught by Ken Boa. Used with permission.

6. This introduction borrows from the teachings of Ken Boa, especially chapters 1–3 of *Conformed to His Image*.

7. This definition comes from Ken Boa.

8. Elisabeth Elliot, ed., *The Journals of Jim Elliot* (Grand Rapids MI: Fleming H. Revell, Baker Book House, 1978), 174.

9. Rick Warren, *The Purpose Driven Life: What on Earth Am I Here For?* (Grand Rapids, MI: Zondervan, 2002), 149.

10. Lewis, *Mere Christianity,* 134.

11. From notes on an in-person study taught by Ken Boa. Used with permission.

12. Blaise Pascal, Pensées, part III, §233.

[13] According to Ken Boa, one compelling reason for this view is that Revelation 19 tells us the marriage of the Lamb takes place prior to Jesus' second advent as King of kings. Since Jesus' bride is the church, this means that this feast must occur prior to his second coming, and the church will come with him to rule and reign in his kingdom.

[14] Augustine, *The Confessions of St. Augustine of Hippo,* LeaderU.com, accessed February 16, 2021, www.leaderu.com/cyber/books/augconfessions/bk1.html.

[15] This prayer is a template commonly suggested by the late Reverend Billy Graham.

ILLUSTRATIONS
BY STEPHEN CROTTS

ABOUT THE AUTHOR

Clearly, John Matthew is a pseudonym, but it is certainly an appropriate one; almost all of the recorded words of Jesus are found in either (or both) of these important Gospels of the New Testament. The identity of the author of this manuscript is unimportant. His objective in creating this manuscript is to help fulfill the Great Commission, and all proceeds from this publication will be used to further its distribution.

"I am the way, and the truth, and the life. No one comes to the Father except through me."
(John 14:6)

⁂

"I am the resurrection and the life. Whoever believes in me, though he die, yet shall he live, and everyone who lives and believes in me shall never die. Do you believe this?"
(John 11:25–26)